Meet My Friend

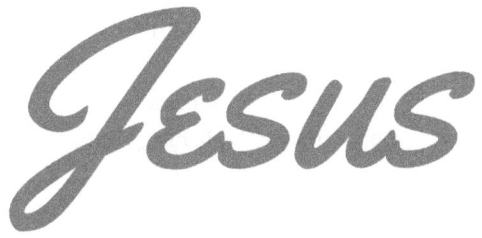

Connecting with Jesus
Through Friendship
and Conversation

TRACY FREDERICK

Copyright © 2019

Tracy Frederick
Performance Publishing Group
McKinney, TX

All Worldwide Rights Reserved.
All rights reserved. No part of this publication may be reproduced, stored in a retrieval system or transmitted, in any form or by any means, electronic, mechanical, recorded, photocopied, or otherwise, without the prior written permission of the copyright owner, except by a reviewer who may quote brief passages in a review.

ISBN 13: 978-1-946629-44-9
ISBN 10: 1-946629-44-8

Contents

Introduction 1

Chapter 1:
Beginning a Friendship with Jesus 5

Chapter 2:
The Importance of Having a Relationship with Jesus 13

Chapter 3:
Preparing for a Conversation with Jesus 23

Chapter 4:
Start Talking 31

Introduction

I have many friends, and you probably do, too. Whether we are gathering for lunch, enjoying a cup of coffee, or celebrating an occasion, it is always fun to be with them. We joke around, laugh at something silly we did together, or cry on each other's shoulder. We bond over the years by sharing our stories and making memories.

I have one friend who I trust with my deepest thoughts, knowing that he will never share my innermost secrets. Having someone to listen and not judge is a big deal for me. No one wants to be ridiculed for their past mistakes and biggest failures. When I go for a long car ride and don't want to be alone, my friend is the perfect travel partner. I talk; he listens. He talks; I listen.

Sometimes we explore the wide open waters that never seem to end, talking about nothing important, just spending time together. Other times we may go for long walks on scenic trails where beauty will take us miles away with only memories of our loved ones that are no longer with us. I often seek his advice, and he is always willing to listen. He will compliment me when I look nice and will also remind me to never wear that again! Some days it's the humor that my friend offers that makes me smile.

There are many days that I wake with excitement, ready to share my most recent thoughts and dreams with my friend. My heart beats with joy knowing that he, too, is happy for me. Friends help each other when they are in need and support each other when life is not okay. There is no better way to connect with a friend than by sharing a prayer to help us get through the day. When I can't find a solution to my unanswered questions, it is my friend who gently reminds me that my prayers are being heard and that the answers will arrive with perfect timing.

What I like about my friend the most is that he is dependable, always on time and never late. He lives in my heart and stays on my mind. He hears me when I call him and enjoys spending time with me, too. My friend is not pushy and never goes where he is not wanted. I am important to him; this he has told me many times. I believe him, for he has never lied to me. He only speaks the truth and waits for me to respond. I love my friend with all my heart. I want you to meet him.

Come with me. I want to introduce you to my friend, Jesus.

Chapter 1

Beginning a Friendship with Jesus

Exodus 33:12 (NIV) I know you by name and you have found favor with me.

We appreciate the time we spend with our friends, and we believe what they tell us is true. Our friends make us laugh or cry, and we love them and want to be with them. There is nothing better than having a best friend with whom you can trust to share all of life's details. That is the same kind of friendship you can have with Jesus. He is compassionate, just as loving as your other friends, and He, too, wants to spend time with you.

When we get introduced to someone, we almost instantly get a feeling of like or dislike. Our mind starts to think, "Hmmm." But as the conversation goes on, we start to take an interest in this new person. We enjoy our time talking and getting to know one another. We soon find out that we have a lot in common: other friends, hobbies, and home life. After our conversation has ended, our minds are made up. Yes, I like this person. Before long, you find yourself wanting to spend time with your new friend. You begin making plans to see each other more often, and a lasting friendship starts to form. You smile at the mention of this person's name. You are happy and excited that you will see your friend again. Remember how easy and effortless it was to make a new friend? Not hard at all, right?

Your willingness to seek Jesus is all you need to begin a friendship with Him. Call Him by name. Talk to Him as you would an old friend. You don't have to be eloquent with your words. Your other friends would think you were strange if you acted that way with them. You are not trying out for a part in an upcoming play by giving an outstanding performance. You are just having a conversation. Talk to Jesus like you would your other friends. Be relaxed. Be yourself. No need to pretend to be someone you are not. Jesus already knows your name. He knows everything about you. It's time to get to know Him.

My Friend Has a Nickname

I don't know about you, but a lot of my friends have nicknames, too. Think of someone that you know who has a formal name like Charles or Susan. You probably call them by the shorter version such as Charlie or Sue. This seems more casual, friendly, and comfortable for you. My Jesus has a nickname, too. I call Him "G." I use this name to call Him just like I would one of my other friends. My friend JoAnn calls him "JC" (Jesus Christ). While another friend calls Him "Bud." These nicknames are informal, and I find it easier to relax and be more open and honest. He hears me every time I call Him by this name. Jesus doesn't care what you call Him. He will recognize your voice and know that it's you! Talk to Him as a friend, not as a boss or someone with authority.

Our true friends are always happy to hear from us. They answer our call with a cheerful "Hello." We hug each other when we meet, and there is an emotion that makes our hearts beat with joy. We can have these same warm feelings when we greet Jesus. He is available twenty-four hours a day, seven days a week. Jesus is always there: at night when you can't sleep and in the morning when you first wake up. He is waiting to hear the sweet sound of His name being called.

Are You Afraid to Talk to Jesus?

Psalm 27:8 (NLT) My heart has heard you say, "Come and talk with me." And my heart responds, "Lord, I am coming."

Being embarrassed often keeps us from talking to Jesus. It took me a long time to realize that He already knew my sins and that asking for forgiveness was His way of healing me and showing me how to move forward. What a relief to no longer carry the weight of my worries. Little did I know that freedom was only a conversation away.

Are you afraid of being judged for the mistakes or bad choices that you have made? Fear not, for Jesus is waiting to hear from you. This is the moment to put aside those thoughts. Let go of the fear and shame that you may possess by being honest, telling Jesus everything you think and feel. Sometimes we can't help but fear that what we tell our friend today might turn into tomorrow's gossip. A friendship with Jesus will assure you that your thoughts are always private and your secrets will never be shared with anyone. Think about it. Have you ever heard someone say Jesus told me what you said? No. He values our friendship and wants our trust.

As you talk about your concerns with Jesus, your fear and anxiety will slowly find its place—out of reach from worry. You will have no regrets when talking to Him first. These conversations will bring peace and joy, knowing that He will always be there to listen. Your confidence in Jesus will grow, and your friendship will be nourished.

It's About a Relationship, Not Religion

You don't have to be a religious person or belong to a church to have a relationship with Jesus. Church is where you meet people and hang out with those that have a relationship with Jesus, too. It's the perfect place to learn more about Him. Many of my friends attend a different church than I do, and some don't go to church at all. This doesn't make you a bad person or less thought of by Jesus. You are worthy just as you are! I spent many months nourishing my friendship with Jesus, every morning and on Sundays, right in my living room. Once you have a relationship with Jesus, you will want to share your experiences with others as well. If I had not had a friendship with Him, I would still be stuck on the couch trying to figure out where I belong.

Chapter 2

The Importance of Having a Relationship with Jesus

Having a friendship with Jesus gives us the freedom to express our thoughts without explanation because He knows us, and He understands us, and He loves us anyway! It is this kind of freedom that gives us the confidence to become the person He designed us to be. We can confide in Jesus, the one friend who willingly listens to our troubles and carries our burdens so we don't have to. Our other friends can hear our frustrations, but He will help us through the difficult days and tragic moments of our lives. It is important to have someone to console us when the bad times arrive on short notice, and it's nice to celebrate the small steps of progress with the One who gave us the courage to try something new. Jesus wants to know the things that happen in everyday situations that bring us joy. Our happiness and success are the gifts He wants us to have. Who better to share these pleasures with than Jesus? You are valued by Jesus, and the only way to know your worth to Him is to have an everlasting relationship with Him.

What's in It for Me?

Jeremiah 29:11 (NLT) "For I know the plans that I have for you," says the Lord. "They are plans for good and not for disaster, to give you a future and a hope."

As our friendship with Jesus develops, we will begin to realize that He is with us every moment of our lives. This is what keeps me from feeling alone. Without this relationship, we are on our own to figure things out. I don't know about you, but I don't always have the right answers. This may be where you are right now: frustrated, tired, and scared of making the wrong choices. You go through each day haphazardly, up one minute and down the next, with no real sense of peace or confirmation as to where your life is headed. Troubling times find you, and you are not sure what to do or how to act to make your life better. When we have a relationship with Jesus, these kinds of thoughts and days won't go away, but we will be better equipped to handle them. Jesus will never leave you. Your belief in Him will grow through daily conversation, and you will learn to live in the present moment by trusting your new friend.

We experience Jesus' goodness by spending time with Him. And when He is ready, He reveals His plan for us at a pace that we can endure. He doesn't want us to miss the lessons or the many blessings He has in store for us. By talking with Jesus, we gain strength in our conversations and restore faith in our future. You may not be able to see what He is doing in your life, but trust Him by believing that He will change your circumstances in order to show you the life He has planned for you.

Will Jesus Hear Me?

Psalm 4:3 (NIV) Know that the Lord has set apart his faithful servant for himself; the Lord hears when I call to him.

You can believe this because Jesus knows your voice, and He is waiting to hear from you. It's no different than when we call our other friends by their names. They recognize our voice, say "Hi," and then the conversation begins. Speak the name Jesus and begin talking. It's that simple! You can talk out loud or silently to yourself. I promise He will hear you. Don't worry about what your other friends will think. At this moment, it is only you and your friend, Jesus. I don't have to be on my knees for Jesus to hear me. He hears me right where I am, whether I am at home or the gym or in the carpool line. I never miss an opportunity to say, "Hello." The more

I talk to Him, the different ways in which He chooses to reveal himself become clear to me.

It's always a relief when I unload my burdens to one of my friends. Jesus is the One who wants to hear it all. So I tell Him when I am stressed out at work or when there's not enough hours in the day to get everything done. I may not get the same reply as I would from another friend, but knowing that He heard me makes me feel better. Don't spare the details when talking to Jesus. He loves hearing us speak with excitement, especially when sharing good news ... like the time when I happened upon a sale and brought home a bargain. I could almost see Him smiling and shaking His head while He was laughing!

If you are having a hard time connecting with Jesus, be persistent. Remind yourself of the many ways that He has helped your friends, other people that you know, or miracles that you have heard about. He wants to do the same for you. He longs to answer our questions and clear up any unresolved issues when there seems to be no solution.

Will Jesus Talk Back to Me?

Jeremiah 33:3 (NLT) Ask me and I will tell you remarkable secrets you do not know about things to come.

Jesus has his own timetable, and it is completely different from ours. He does not get in a hurry and neither should we. There is no major decision that has to be made on the spur of the moment. None!

He will answer you when the time is right and you are ready to hear what he has to say. I have to admit, He doesn't always answer me immediately after I ask a question. Be patient. Enjoy each day while you wait in joyful anticipation for His reply.

Jesus works in simplicity. He is not going to crowd our minds full of "what ifs." He is not going to fill our heads with doubt, but He will show us how to shift our perspective so that we see our situation through His eyes.

It would be so easy if He would just show up by walking through the door, sit down, and talk to us face to face, but that's not how it happens. When you really need an answer or you are desperate to hear from Jesus, find a calm quiet place where you can connect with Him.

You should know that the answers that you are looking for may come from Jesus' gentle voice or other unexpected sources. More than likely, they probably will be spoken to you through someone else. Jesus uses the voices of others to carry His messages. Be listening for the many ways in which He will talk to you. It could be through a conversation with a friend or a stranger, as well as the words to a song or even a TV commercial. You never know where you will be or who you will be with when you hear the voice of Jesus.

One day I was journaling a letter to Jesus. I had thoughts of a new house and a different neighborhood on my mind. A few days later, I was driving along, and I heard the words, "Don't wish for what you don't have." That may not be the answer to your prayer, but it certainly was mine. I have not thought of moving since that day a few years ago!

Chapter 3

Preparing for a Conversation with Jesus

Jesus wants us in His life, and He wants to be an important part of ours. Talking with Him is an acceptable form of prayer, and the greatest part is that we get to decide when and where we hold our conversations as well as what we are going to talk about. When you want to talk to your other friends, you pick up the phone and make the call. It's that easy with Jesus, too. He will never not answer your call, cry, or plea. You only need the desire to speak to Him and the willingness to talk to start a conversation.

Do you want to have a conversation with Jesus? If so, here are some ways that you can prepare.

Choose a Place to Talk to Jesus

Where are you when you talk to your other friends? You can meet Jesus at those same places: a coffee shop, at your house, or on a park bench. It doesn't matter. He is going to show up wherever **you** choose. Pick a place that makes you feel comfortable so you can enjoy your conversation. It may be your bedroom or an office. For me, it's my favorite chair.

Jesus loves to travel. When I vacation, whether I am arriving by car, bus, or plane, I always ask Him to be the co-pilot. We can talk to Him anywhere from Disney World to Denmark. He likes the beach as well as the mountains, the open road, or the raging sea. Prison cells and palaces. He's been there, too. There is not a seat that He can't fit in or a room that can't hold Him. He goes wherever we go.

Jesus met many of His followers in unexpected places. What they were wearing and where they sat was the least of His concerns. He only wanted their attention so that He could talk to them.

Choose a Time to Talk to Jesus

There is no right time, bad time, or perfect time to talk to Jesus. It's anytime! However, by setting aside a time every day, you will form a habit of thinking about Him and looking forward to your time together. For me, morning works best while drinking coffee and gathering my first thoughts. Others prefer to wait until evening to tell Jesus about their day. Because He is always available, we don't have to worry about choosing the wrong time to start our conversation. If, for whatever reason, you have to pause your conversation, it's okay. He will patiently wait for you to return, even if it's hours later.

Some days there just isn't time for a sit down conversation. I often think of something I want to say, but I don't have time to stop what I am doing and talk. That's fine with Jesus. On those days, jump right in and start talking. You won't surprise Him, and He will never tell you that He's not ready. That happens to me when I have an early morning appointment. It's all I can do to get myself ready and out the door. He knows that we are busy, and He would rather us talk to Him on the spur of the moment than to dismiss Him altogether.

Choose the Right Mindset to Talk to Jesus

Matthew 7:7 (NIV) Ask, and it will be given to you; seek and you will find; knock and the door will be opened to you.

I often prepare myself spiritually before I begin my conversation with Jesus. I do this because it helps me to clear my mind and think only of Him. This also helps me to concentrate on what I want to say, and it puts me in a better frame of mind to hear from Him. I choose to do one or more of the following:

- Read a devotional before starting my conversation. Sometimes I visualize myself in the situation that's being described. It reminds me to ask Jesus to help me in that area as well. Knowing that He has helped others and believing that He will help me, too, gives me a sense of hope. This also gives me courage to ask for my own wants and needs.

- Read my Bible. I can choose any book of the Bible and find stories and lessons to be learned. There, I will also find words of truth along with knowledge and wisdom. I like to see the areas in which I relate to the men and women that Jesus ministered to so long ago. Through these pages, I learn the many ways that Jesus spoke to others.

- Journal my thoughts instead of talking. This is my favorite way to connect with Jesus. I write His name according to what I want to call Him that day (Father, Jesus, or G). For me, it's easier to explain what I want to say or ask. He doesn't judge me for my punctuation or spelling! He hears me just the same. I like to reflect on my writings and see the ways that Jesus chooses to deliver me through the difficult situations as well as the blessings He has bestowed upon me. If you can't speak it, you can write it.

It's up to you how you choose to start your conversation. But you can rely on this one truth: He is waiting to hear from you.

Chapter 4

Start Talking

There is no better time or place to start your conversation than right now, where you are at this very moment.

Jesus is the one friend who really wants to hear it all, so tell Him anything and everything. Sometimes we choose our place and time to talk to Jesus, and then we become lost for words. There is so much we want to say that we don't know where to begin. We get so consumed with our thoughts beforehand that when the time comes, we find ourselves powerless to speak. On those days, I start with simple thoughts like these:

- I tell Jesus that I love Him. This warms His heart and pleases Him dearly. I also tell Him about the other people in my life that I love, and I ask Him to grant a favor or well wish on my behalf. He loves a generous heart that thinks of others.

- I ask Jesus to forgive me for the wrong things that I have said, thought, and done. I remind Jesus the ways in which I have been selfish: forgetting others, being unsympathetic to those in need, or thinking of only myself. I then ask Him to help me improve. There are many others that have had these same faults. He has willingly forgiven them, and He will forgive me, too.

- I offer words of thanks and praise by remembering all the good things that He has given to me. Not only the gifts that I drive, store in my closet, or wear on my back, but the talents and abilities that have been bestowed upon me—the ones that I know about and the ones that I don't. Jesus loves a thankful heart.

When my days are filled with too many emotions to utter any words, I become still and listen. I close my eyes, take a deep breath, and let Jesus start the conversation. Quietly, I listen for the light whisper of His voice. I may hear Him call my name, or I may hear nothing at all, only the peace and stillness of the moment giving me the opportunity to say what's on my mind. And then there are the days that I am ready to talk, and it's easy to go from minutes to hours with my conversation. On those days I tell it all, starting at the top, stopping only to breathe fresh air. After all, that's what I do with my other friends.

There are many other conversations that you can have with Jesus. You can share with Him the secret desires of your heart: the position at work that you want, the perfect spouse for you, or the simple pleasure of a nice vacation.

Is there something that has caused you pain? It may be a health issue, a broken relationship, or a loss of a loved one. Share it with Jesus and let Him show you how to be healed.

Don't forget about the little victories of a routine day, the ones that go without incident or problem. Things such as light traffic, getting to work on time, or enjoying a good meal. Jesus wants to hear about these moments, too.

Relationships with our friends can sometimes be difficult. We fear being judged for the decisions we have made or the unkind words that we have spoken and can't take back. These conversations are hard to have with someone we care about, but these are the things that Jesus wants to hear from us. He wants to know about the people in our lives who have been unkind to us, as well as the people we have hurt. Ask Him to restore the friendship if that is His desire. If you have doubts about your partner or spouse, express your thoughts. He once let me know that the root cause of a situation was my pride. It was **my** perspective that needed to change! I always talk about my children, asking Him to bless them with a future filled with His will not mine. He reminds me on a regular basis that He made each one of us unique, and my children are not always going to think or act like me.

It really doesn't matter to Jesus what we talk about first or last. His interest will always be the same. If it's important to you, it will be important to Him.

Jesus knows what is going on in our lives, but He wants to hear our side of the story. Exhale, introduce yourself to Jesus, and start talking!

Romans 5:11 (NLT) So now we can rejoice in our wonderful new relationship with God because our Lord Jesus Christ has made us friends with God.

Thank you for reading!
If you would like to order more copies
to share with your friends,
you can contact me at
tracy@tracyfrederick.net

www.ingramcontent.com/pod-product-compliance
Lightning Source LLC
Chambersburg PA
CBHW070803050426
42452CB00012B/2474